DK SUPER Planet

A Journey Around our CONTINENTS

Explore the seven continents that make up our planet,
and discover the incredible landscapes
and environments of each one

Produced for DK by
Editorial Just Content Limited
Design Studio Noel

Author Nancy Raines Day

Senior Editor Amelia Jones
Senior Art Editor Gilda Pacitti
Managing Editor Katherine Neep
Managing Art Editor Sarah Corcoran
Production Editor Jaypal Chauhan
DTP Designer Rohit Singh
Production Controller Rebecca Parton
Publisher Sarah Forbes
Managing Director, Learning Hilary Fine

First American Edition, 2025
Published in the United States by DK Publishing,
a division of Penguin Random House LLC
1745 Broadway, 20th Floor, New York, NY 10019

A catalog record for this book
is available from the Library of Congress.
HC ISBN: 978-0-5939-6602-0
PB ISBN: 978-0-5939-6601-3

DK books are available at special discounts when purchased
in bulk for sales promotions, premiums, fund-raising,
or educational use.
For details, contact: DK Publishing Special Markets,
1745 Broadway, 20th Floor, New York, NY 10019
SpecialSales@dk.com

Printed and bound in China

www.dk.com

This book was made with Forest
Stewardship Council™ certified
paper – one small step in DK's
commitment to a sustainable future.
**Learn more at www.dk.com/uk/
information/sustainability**

Contents

Words in **bold** are explained in the glossary on page 44.

The CONTINENTS

A continent is a large area of land. Earth is divided into seven continents. Each continent is unique, with differences in the weather, landscapes, and **cultures**. Let's go on a journey around each of these fascinating continents!

NORTH AMERICA

Greenland is the largest **island** in the world and is part of the North American continent. All the countries in **North America** touch an ocean.

SOUTH AMERICA

The world's largest **rainforest**, the Amazon, is found in **South America**. The rainforest surrounds the mighty Amazon River, which carries more water than any other river in the world.

AFRICA

With 54 countries, **Africa** has the most countries of any continent. Scientists believe that modern humans developed in Africa around 300,000 years ago.

EUROPE

Europe and **Asia** are connected. These two continents are actually part of the same landmass, and together they are sometimes called Eurasia. More of Europe is suitable for farming than any other continent.

ASIA

Over 4.6 billion people live in Asia, which is more than half the world's population. Asia is home to Mount Everest, the tallest mountain on Earth.

AUSTRALIA

The only place in the world that is both a country and a continent, **Australia** is the smallest continent. It is also the flattest and driest inhabited continent, with some of the oldest land **formations** in the world.

ANTARCTICA

During the winter, sea ice forms around **Antarctica**, doubling its size. Millions of years ago, Antarctica was not covered in ice. It used to be warm and full of plants and animals.

Introduction to
NORTH AMERICA

The continent of North America stretches from **tropical** Panama to the Arctic Circle. Since it is in the Northern **Hemisphere**, the summer is from June to August. Canada, the United States of America, and Mexico are the largest of North America's 23 countries. North America is home to sweeping forests, wide **plains**, vast **deserts**, huge mountains, and incredible rock formations.

The Inuit people live in Nunavut, in the Canadian Arctic. The Canadian Arctic makes up around 40 percent of Canada's land mass. Apart from some small **settlements**, the vast landscape is largely **unpopulated** by humans, but is home to a wide variety of wildlife, including polar bears, wolves, arctic foxes, seals, and whales.

The Maya people built this pyramid over 1,000 years ago. It is part of Chichén Itzá, an area of Maya **ruins** in Mexico, and is a symbol of the rich Maya culture. Maya people are the **ancestors** of many Mexicans.

The Golden Gate Bridge is a famous **landmark**. It is located in the San Francisco Bay on the west **coast** of America. The distinctive orange color of the bridge makes it clearly visible to ships in foggy weather.

Find out!

Choose one of the island countries of North America. What can you find out about its history and its government?

The West Indies are an island group in North America. They contain over 7,000 islands, the largest being Cuba. They were named by Christopher Columbus, a navigator who explored the Americas in the 15th century, who thought he had reached India. They are now also known as the Caribbean.

Toronto is in the province of Ontario. It is the biggest city in Canada, and almost 3 million Canadians live there. The city skyline is dominated by the CN Tower, which is 1,815 ft (553 m) tall and was once the tallest freestanding structure in the world.

Exploring NORTH AMERICA

The United States of America is one of the largest countries in the world. The US mainland stretches about 2,800 miles (4,500 km) from east to west. Jamaica is an island located to the east of Central America. It is the third largest island in the West Indies, but the whole island is smaller than the US state of Connecticut.

Many American children learn to play musical instruments in band class. Popular school sports include football, basketball, track and field, baseball, and soccer.

The US has 48 **contiguous** states. Alaska, which touches Canada, and Hawaii, in the Pacific Ocean, make it 50 states. The US also has several **territories** in other parts of the world, including American Samoa, Guam, the Northern Mariana Islands, Puerto Rico, and the US Virgin Islands.

The American West is known for its wide, open spaces and astounding **landforms**. That includes the Grand Canyon in Arizona, which is a popular spot with hikers.

The Statue of Liberty is a famous landmark in New York Harbor. New York City is on the US East Coast. The statue is a figure of Libertas, the Roman goddess of liberty, and it represents freedom. It was a gift from France, given to the US in 1885.

Fascinating fact

Both the US and Jamaica celebrate independence days. Americans celebrate on July 4, and Jamaicans celebrate on August 6.

Kingston

The largest city and capital of Jamaica is Kingston. It is a coastal city known for its beautiful scenery and natural **harbor**. It is home to Hope Gardens, one of the largest botanical gardens in the West Indies.

Jamaica is famous for its reggae music, which originated there in the 1960s. Its popularity then spread around the world.

Introduction to
SOUTH AMERICA

South America stretches from around the **equator** to close to Antarctica, but it is smaller in size than North America. It has 12 countries, including Brazil and Chile. Since it is mostly in the Southern Hemisphere, summer is from January to March. South America is home to tropical rainforests, dry deserts, and high **mountain ranges**.

The Andes

The Andes is a mountain range that runs about 5,500 miles (8,900 km) along South America's west coast. It is the world's longest mountain range above ground. It contains glaciers, volcanoes, forests, lakes, deserts, and **grasslands**.

The Victoria Amazonica water lily can be found in South America. It grows enormous pads, up to 10 ft (3 m) across.

The **ancient** ruins at Machu Picchu in Peru were studied and restored in the early 1900s. The Incas built this vast settlement in the 1400s. It was the palace of Pachacuti Inca Yupanqui, an Incan ruler.

The Amazon River is at least 4,000 miles (6,400 km) long. It winds around the Amazon, which is the world's largest tropical rainforest. It is mostly located in Brazil and contains millions of species of plants and animals.

La Paz is Bolivia's capital. It is located on the Andean **plateau**, more than 2 miles (3.65 km) above sea level. This makes it the world's highest national capital. Tourists visiting La Paz can have trouble catching their breath, since it is located at such a high **elevation**. It is full of markets like this one.

Exploring
SOUTH AMERICA

Brazil is a huge country on the east coast of South America. Colombia is a much smaller country located in the northwest of the continent. The Andes Mountains run north to south right through it. Brazil also has many mountains, especially in the south. The Amazon Rainforest spans both countries.

Portuguese is the official language of Brazil. Many Portuguese settlers moved to Brazil, starting in the 1500s. Brazilians also speak many **Indigenous** and European languages.

Christ the Redeemer is a famous landmark that overlooks the Brazilian city of Rio de Janeiro. The statue is 98 ft (30 m) tall. Like Machu Picchu in Peru, Christ the Redeemer has been voted one of the New Seven Wonders of the World.

Carnival is celebrated every year across the continent. Many South American children like to dress up and watch the parade of dancers with family and friends. The biggest carnival is celebrated in Rio de Janeiro, and millions of people participate.

Find out!

Can you find out which South American country is named after Simón Bolívar?

Bolivia.

Spanish is the official language of Colombia. This is because many Spanish settlers moved to Colombia, starting in the 16th century. There are also around 65 Indigenous languages spoken in Colombia.

This statue of Simón Bolívar is in the Colombian city of Cartagena. Simón Bolívar was a military officer from Venezuela. Known as "the liberator," he won independence for Colombia and five other countries from Spain.

Introduction to
AFRICA

Africa is the only continent that is partly covered by each of the four hemispheres. One billion people live in the 54 countries here. Africa is home to hot deserts, tropical rainforests, grasslands, and snowy mountains. It supports a huge variety of wildlife that is not found anywhere else on Earth.

Madagascar is an island off the east coast of Africa. About nine-tenths of all the plants and animals that live here are not found anywhere else on Earth, such as the ring-tailed lemur.

Madagascar

Herds of African elephants search for food on the **savanna**. Elephants are the largest living land animals, and an adult elephant can weigh as much as a stack of seven cars.

Giraffes roam Africa's grasslands in places such as Serengeti National Park in Tanzania. With their long necks, giraffes are able to feed on the leaves of tall trees like acacia. Each giraffe has unique markings, in a similar way to human fingerprints.

You will also find lions in Africa's grasslands. Lions live in groups called prides. A pride can have as many as 40 lions living together. Groups of female lions usually hunt together. Lions rest and sleep for 20 hours a day and hunt at night.

Mountain gorillas can only be found in three countries: the Democratic Republic of Congo, Rwanda, and Uganda. They were previously classed as critically **endangered**, but due to **conservation** efforts their population has increased in recent years.

Exploring
AFRICA

Egypt is in North Africa, in the Northern Hemisphere. Though most of it is covered by the Sahara Desert, it is also home to the famous Nile River. The land around the Nile is green and **fertile**. Tanzania is in Eastern Africa, in the Southern Hemisphere. It is full of grasslands, tropical rainforests, and mountains.

The Nile River is over 4,000 miles (6,800 km) long. More than 95 percent of Egypt's population rely on its water and live within a few miles of the river banks.

The pyramids of Giza are important **monuments** of the ancient Egyptian **civilization**. They were built around 4,500 years ago. The Great Sphinx of Giza depicts a mythological creature that has the head of a human and the body of a lion.

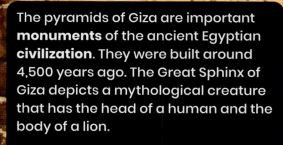

Bedouins are **nomadic** people who live in the desert, including in Egypt. Many people herd animals, like sheep and camels.

Cairo is Egypt's capital and the largest city in Africa. Around 10 million people live there. It has a fascinating mix of old and new buildings.

Once a small fishing village, Dar es Salaam is now Tanzania's biggest city and home to over 5 million people. With a diverse population, the city is a blend of African, Arab, and European influences.

Tanzania is home to many Indigenous people who have unique cultures and traditions, including the Maasai people. They are traditionally herders and **barter** cattle in exchange for other things.

Mount Kilimanjaro in Tanzania is the highest mountain in Africa. It is actually a volcano, but it is dormant which means it is not going to erupt any time soon.

Introduction to
EUROPE

Europe is in the Northern Hemisphere. It has 44 countries. In the north are the Nordic countries including Sweden and Denmark, which extend up to the Arctic Circle. In the south, countries including Greece and Malta border the Mediterranean Sea. Europe is home to snowy mountain ranges, deep rivers, and conifer forests.

Fascinating fact

Vatican City is the world's smallest country. It is located inside of Rome, in Italy. It has an area of 0.19 sq miles (0.49 sq km).

The Alps

Vatican City

European hedgehogs are fou... throughout Western Europe. They are friends of gardeners since they eat different gard... pests. They hibernate during the coldest months of the ye...

The Alps are a large mountain range in the middle of Europe. Around 30 million people visit the Alps each year to enjoy activities such as skiing, snowboarding, and hiking.

European pine martens can be found throughout the continent. They make their dens in holes in old trees. They are mainly active at dusk and at night.

The Eiffel Tower is one of the most famous sights of the Paris skyline in France. It was completed in 1889. It stands 984 ft (300 m) high.

Sitting on a hill above the Greek city of Athens, the Acropolis is a monument to the achievements of the ancient Greeks. The most famous building is the Parthenon. It was built almost 2,500 years ago.

Exploring
EUROPE

The United Kingdom (UK) is made up of England, Wales, Scotland, and Northern Ireland. The UK is home to many woodlands, wetlands, and mountains. Italy is closer to the equator and generally has a warm climate. It has many hills, mountains, and forests. Both countries have beautiful coastal areas. Although Italy is a bit bigger, the UK has a larger population.

Giant's Causeway is in Northern Ireland. The area is made up of a landform known as a **limestone pavement**. It formed as a result of ancient volcanic activity.

This famous clock tower can be found at the Houses of Parliament in London, England. It is commonly called Big Ben, but that is actually the name of the bell inside. The tower's official name is the Elizabeth Tower, named after Queen Elizabeth II.

Conwy Castle is in Wales. It was built in the 1200s on a coastal ridge at an important crossing point over the River Conwy. It is a UNESCO World Heritage site.

Fascinating fact

The Colosseum is one of Italy's 60 UNESCO World Heritage sites. These are places around the world of great historical importance. Italy has more UNESCO sites than any other country.

The Colosseum was built in the first century. It hosted **gladiator** battles, **chariot** races, and other spectacles in ancient Rome.

Lake Como is found at the foothills of the Alps. It is the third largest lake in Italy. It is known for its beautiful scenery and elegant villas, and is a popular tourist destination.

Gelato is a very popular frozen treat in Italy. It is a lot like ice cream. You can buy it at gelaterias and cafés.

Introduction to
ASIA

Asia is the largest continent in the Northern and Eastern Hemispheres. It makes up nearly one-third of all land on Earth. China and India are two of the biggest of Asia's 48 countries. The continent has a huge variety of landscapes, from frozen **tundra** to tropical rainforests, and high mountains to low valleys.

The Caspian Sea is a huge inland sea in Central Asia. It is considered the largest lake in the world. It has a surface area of 143,200 sq miles (371,000 sq km).

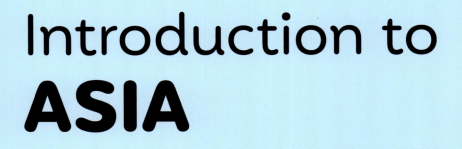

The Maldives is the smallest country in Asia. It is a group of around 1,200 islands located in the Indian Ocean, off the coast of Sri Lanka. The white sandy beaches and spectacular coral reefs bring a lot of **tourism** to the islands.

Almost one-fifth of the world's rainforests are found in Southeast Asia. They are some of the oldest on Earth. The rainforests in Malaysia may have existed over 100 million years ago.

Find out!

Can you find Asia on a globe? How many of its countries can you name?

Snow leopards thrive in the cold, high mountains across Northern and Central Asia. Their large paws act like snowshoes, helping them walk on the snow.

In the wild, giant pandas only live in the mountains of South Central China. They eat bamboo shoots and leaves. Giant pandas are good swimmers and excellent tree climbers.

Exploring ASIA

When it comes to population, India and China are the top two countries in the world. Both have over 1 billion residents! But in terms of area, China is about three times bigger than India. Both countries have cool, dry deserts as well as hot, wet rainforests.

Children light clay lamps to celebrate Diwali. This festival of lights celebrates banishing the darkness of winter.

The Taj Mahal in India is famous around the world for its beautiful **architecture**. It attracts more than 7 million visitors a year.

Mumbai is India's most populous city. It has a thriving movie industry, producing movies in the Hindi language.

The Forbidden City is in the heart of Beijing, which is China's largest and capital city. Originally the emperor's palace, it is a museum today.

In Beijing, children practice lion dancing for the New Year parade. Lunar New Year celebrates spring. It is an important holiday in China.

The Great Wall of China winds for around 13,000 miles (21,000 km) from China's east coast, across mountains to deserts in the west.

Fascinating fact

Sections of the Great Wall of China have bricks held together by mortar made from sticky rice.

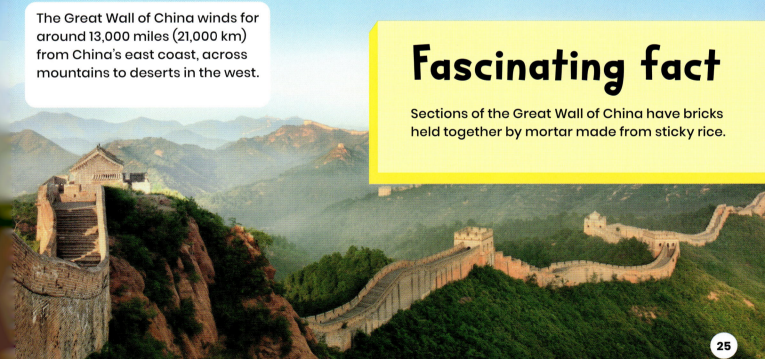

Introduction to
AUSTRALIA

Australia is the smallest continent on Earth. Besides the country of Australia, it includes New Zealand and many islands in the Pacific Ocean, such as Papua New Guinea. Australia is in the Southern Hemisphere. It has everything from snowy mountains to deserts, rainforests, and grasslands. It also has some of the most unusual plant and animal species on the planet.

Fiji is a group of islands in the southern Pacific Ocean. Its main industry is tourism, but Fiji also produces clothing, sugar, fish, and gold.

Little penguins are the world's smallest penguin, and the only penguin with blue and white feathers. They are found in New Zealand and Australia.

Koalas live in eucalyptus trees in Australia. Like kangaroos, mothers can carry their babies in a pouch.

Uluru is a rock formation in the Australian Outback. It is sacred to the local **Aboriginal** people, the Aṇangu people. A cultural center near the base of Uluru teaches visitors about the **society** and culture of Aboriginal people.

The purinina, also known as the Tasmanian devil, is found on the island state of Tasmania. It is a marsupial, related to koalas and kangaroos. Purininas use their long whiskers and excellent sense of smell and sight to hunt and to avoid predators.

Exploring
AUSTRALIA

Over 26 million people live in Australia, mostly around the coast. Papua New Guinea is much smaller, with a population of around 11 million. Australia contains dry deserts, savannas, forests, swamps, and more. Papua New Guinea is mostly mountains and tropical rainforest.

Australian Rules football is a contact sport that is similar to rugby. It is the most popular sport in Australia.

Didgeridoos are wind instruments. They were first invented over 1,000 years ago. They are used in Aboriginal dances and ceremonies.

Water sports, such as sailing, are popular pastimes in Australia.

Sing-sings are an important part of the culture in Papua New Guinea. Performers paint themselves and wear special costumes for these traditional dances.

Women across Papua New Guinea weave colorful bilum bags out of string. The practice is handed down from generation to generation.

When Papua New Guinea gained its independence from Australia in 1975, Port Moresby was made its capital.

Fascinating fact

Papua New Guinea has over 830 living languages. One of the official languages is a **creole** language called Tok Pisin. It is a blend of English and Indigenous languages.'

Introduction to **ANTARCTICA**

Antarctica surrounds the South Pole. Summer brings almost constant daylight from October to March. Temperatures in summer hover around freezing. Winter brings nearly constant darkness for the other six months, and temperatures can drop as low as −58°F (−50°C).

Fascinating fact

More than 98 percent of this frozen continent is covered in ice.

Orcas are found in the Southern Ocean around Antarctica. They are one of the biggest carnivores on Earth, growing almost 32 ft (10 m) long!

Antarctica is covered in mountains and a sheet of ice. In some places, the ice is almost 3 miles (4.8 km) thick.

In the summer, when the ice melts, you might see one of the two plants that flower in Antarctica: Antarctic hair grass and Antarctic pearlwort. Some lichens and mosses also grow here.

Antarctica is known for its emperor penguins. Emperor penguins live in big groups. Male penguins **incubate** the eggs of their young until they hatch.

Icebergs are a common sight in the sea that surrounds Antarctica. So are fur seals. They eat mostly **krill**, fish, and squid.

Exploring
ANTARCTICA

Antarctica has no countries. But countries from every other continent have research stations there. Countries that have bases there include the US, Argentina, the UK, South Africa, Japan, and Australia. Among the 89 permanent stations, about half are seasonal. There are around 5,000 science and support staff on Antarctica in the summer, and 1,000 in the winter.

These flags represent the first 12 countries to sign the 1959 Antarctic Treaty. Today, 57 countries have signed it. The aim of the treaty is to ensure peaceful international cooperation in scientific research and conservation in Antarctica.

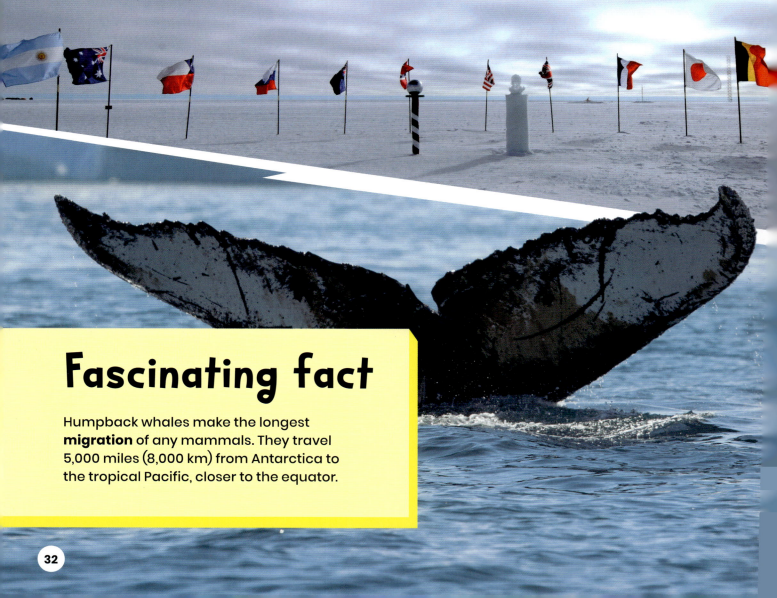

Fascinating fact

Humpback whales make the longest **migration** of any mammals. They travel 5,000 miles (8,000 km) from Antarctica to the tropical Pacific, closer to the equator.

Argentina's Esperanza Base is a permanent research station on Antarctica. It is also one of only two **civilian** settlements on the continent, and families live there year-round. The community has a chapel, a school, a post office, and a medical center.

THE UNITED STATES OF AMERICA
WELCOMES YOU TO
AMUNDSEN – SCOTT SOUTH POLE STATION

The Amundsen-Scott South Pole Station was named after two explorers who raced to be the first to reach the South Pole. Scientists there study glaciers, test telescopes, and conduct medical research.

Everyday
SCIENCE
GPS Navigation

See if you can spot any satellites in the night sky. They look like stars, but they move steadily. They do not twinkle.

If you need to get around on any of Earth's seven continents, it helps to know exactly where you are, and how to get to where you're going. One way you can do this is using the Global Positioning System, or GPS. This works using **satellites** in space.

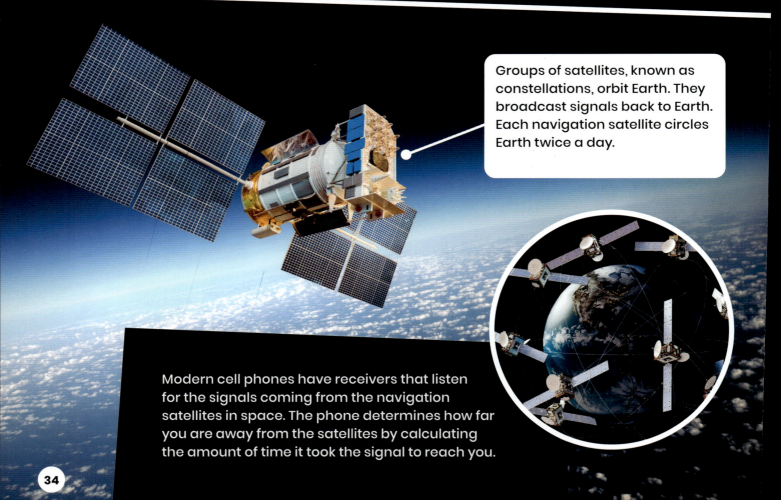

Groups of satellites, known as constellations, orbit Earth. They broadcast signals back to Earth. Each navigation satellite circles Earth twice a day.

Modern cell phones have receivers that listen for the signals coming from the navigation satellites in space. The phone determines how far you are away from the satellites by calculating the amount of time it took the signal to reach you.

Travelers once relied on maps, compasses, and their knowledge of the stars to navigate. Now, we rely on cell phones to show and tell us how to get where we are going.

GPS can be used to track people or objects, give directions to a destination, or provide information about nearby businesses.

Some people also use GPS in their cars. Car navigation systems help drivers get from one point to another.

GPS is used in airplanes, trains, submarines, and even space shuttles.

Everyday **SCIENCE**
Tracking Nature

GPS devices in the ocean can monitor events such as oil spills. Tracking the movement of the oil can help it get cleaned up as soon as possible.

GPS is not just used in navigation. It is also used by scientists around the world. **Ecologists** use GPS to track animals. They can follow an animal's movements to learn about its behavior. And **volcanologists** use GPS to monitor volcanoes. It can help them understand if a volcano might be close to erupting.

Ecologists use special collars to track the movements of wild animals. These collars use GPS. Similar to a cell phone, they contain a receiver that picks up signals from satellites to determine the animal's location.

Ecologists also use GPS to track the flight patterns of birds. Knowing their migration pattern and where the birds stop helps ecologists know which habitats to protect. Tracking has shown us that some birds will even cross several continents on their migration.

Scientists can use GPS to track down animals and make sure they are healthy. They can help animals that are hurt or ill.

Volcanologists monitor the most dangerous volcanoes on Earth. These are volcanoes close to where lots of people live. They want to know if a volcano might erupt so they can warn people.

GPS is one way to monitor volcanoes. GPS receivers are placed around the volcano to track the ground movement. This can help scientists predict when the volcano is going to erupt.'

Let's EXPERIMENT!

FLY A PAPER PLANE

The quickest way to journey around our continents is by flying. In this experiment, you will make your own paper plane. Use the list of things you will need and follow the steps on the right.

You will need:
- 1 piece of 8.5" by 11" paper

1 Fold the piece of paper in half lengthwise to make a crease. Unfold it. Then, fold the two top outer corners into the center crease. This will form a triangle.

Be careful when flying your plane. Fly it somewhere outside.

2 Fold the triangle down. The paper should almost be folded in half. It should look like an envelope.

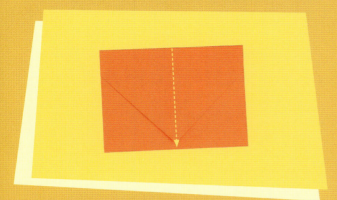

3 Fold each of the top corners down so they meet at the center.

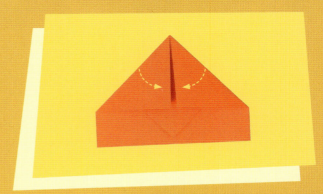

4 Fold the small triangle up. Then, fold the paper in half along the original center crease. The small triangle should be on the outside.

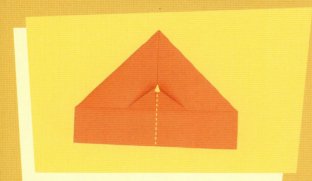

5 Make the wings. Fold down along the dotted line, as shown.

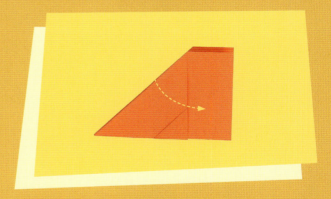

6 Your paper plane is ready for its first flight!

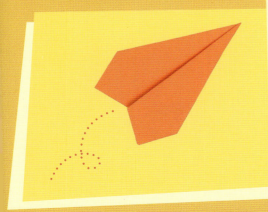

THE WRIGHT BROTHERS' PLANE

The first airplane to take flight was built by brothers Orville and Wilbur Wright. In 1903, they completed four flights in North Carolina, US. The longest one lasted 59 seconds. This photo shows a **replica** of their plane.

Let's EXPERIMENT!

MAKE SUPER HAIL

Sometimes extreme weather hits our continents, such as hailstones. Did you know that you can make your own super-sized hailstones? Use the list of things you will need and follow the steps on the right.

You will need:

- An unopened bottle of spring water
- A bottle of tap water
- A clock or stopwatch
- An ice cube
- A tray or dish
- Access to a freezer

Make sure to remove the tap water from the freezer once it has frozen, otherwise it may explode! Be careful when pouring the cold water. Clean up any spilled water to avoid accidents.

1 Place the bottle of spring water and the bottle of tap water in the freezer. Wait 2 hours. Then, check every 15 minutes to see if the bottle of tap water has frozen.

2 Once the tap water has frozen, take the bottles out of the freezer. Carefully take the top off the bottle of spring water. This will still be in liquid form. That is because ice crystals can form around the dust particles in tap water, but the spring water contains no dust.

3 Place the ice cube on the tray or dish.

4 Pour the supercooled spring water onto the ice cube. Watch it grow!

GIANT HAILSTONES

Hail forms when tiny pieces of dust or ice are blown high into very cold clouds. Cold water droplets in the clouds freeze around the pieces of dust or ice. Eventually, the icy pieces get too heavy to stay up in the air. They fall to the ground as hail.

Vocabulary
BUILDER
Pen Pals

Pen pals are friends who write letters to each other. Having a pen pal can be a great way to find out about the everyday life of someone in another country or continent. You can learn about how their culture and customs are different to yours, or what things you have in common.

Lina and Robeka are pen pals. Lina lives in a town on Colombia's coast. Robeka lives with her Maasai family in Kenya. Here are two letters they sent to each other.

Buenos, Robeka,

I am excited to write to someone who lives on another continent. I found Kenya on our globe at school. We both live near the equator. I live in a small town near the coast. What about you? Is it hot where you live? It gets so hot here. Right now, I am learning to sing and dance to folk music. It is part of my culture. Can you tell me about your customs too?

Write back soon.

Your friend, Lina

Things you do in your country	cook traditional food, go camping, hike, meet up with friends, play a sport or musical instrument, play cards or board games, see a movie, sightsee, spend time with family, study, visit a museum
Things about your country	attractions, clothing, continent, culture, customs, food, hemisphere, landmarks, landscape, monuments, sports, street art, traditions, weather, wildlife

 Sopa, Lina,

I found Colombia on a map at school. You live in the Northern Hemisphere, but I live in the Southern Hemisphere. It is hot and dry here. I just started learning how to make bead jewelry, which is one of our local traditions. Rock art is another ancient tradition here. Our ancestors made pictures of animals like giraffes and elephants. We have amazing wildlife in Kenya! What wildlife is there in your country?

Your pen pal,

Robeka

Imagine you have a pen pal on another continent. Write a letter to them. Think about:

- Where you live
- What is interesting about your country
- What your traditions and hobbies are

Use the words in the vocabulary box above, the examples on pages 42–43, and the prompts to help you.

Glossary

Aboriginal people Indigenous peoples of Australia.

Africa One of the seven continents and the only one that is located in all four hemispheres.

Ancestor Someone who a person or group is descended from.

Ancient Something from a long time ago.

Antarctica One of the seven continents, located in the Southern Hemisphere.

Architecture The design of a building.

Asia One of the seven continents and the largest on Earth.

Australia One of the seven continents and the smallest on Earth.

Barter To trade by exchanging one thing for another without using money.

Bedouin The nomadic tribes who live in deserts across North Africa and Southwest Asia.

Chariot A type of horse-drawn vehicle used in ancient Rome.

Civilian Anyone who is not a member of the military.

Civilization Any human society in the past or present that has culture and technology.

Coast Where the land meets the sea.

Conservation The preservation and protection of a place and its wildlife.

Contiguous Touching each other at a boundary or point, for example two continents that share a border.

Creole A language that develops from a blend of two or more languages.

Culture The way a group of people lives, including their language, clothes, celebrations, and art.

Desert A dry landscape that can be hot or cold and does not have much vegetation.

Ecologist A scientist who studies plants, animals, and their habitats.

Elevation The height of something, such as the distance above sea level.

Endangered At risk of becoming extinct.

Equator The imaginary line that circles Earth from east to west.

Europe One of the seven continents, located in the Northern Hemisphere.

Fertile Land that is good for growing crops.

Formation Something made up of rock that looks different than the other rocks around it.

Gladiator In ancient Rome, a warrior who fought in battles to entertain others.

Grassland A wide and open expanse of grasses, shrubs, and few trees.

Habitat The natural home of an animal or plant.

Hemisphere One of the halves that Earth is divided into—either the Western and Eastern, or the Northern and Southern.

Harbor A protected, deep part of the sea or ocean that is close to land and can be used as a port for ships.

Iceberg A piece of freshwater glacier that has broken off into the ocean.

Incubate To help an egg hatch, often by sitting on it or otherwise keeping it warm.

Indigenous Something that originates from a specific region.

Island A landmass surrounded by sea or ocean on all sides.

Krill A tiny shrimp-like marine animal.

Landform A natural feature on Earth's surface that is part of the land.

Landmark A place of outstanding historic or cultural importance.

Limestone pavement An exposed area of limestone, a type of soft rock, that looks like big, rectangular blocks.

Migration Moving from one place to another, for example when animals travel to another habitat for part of the year.

Monument An important structure that was built long ago.

Mountain range A group of mountains that form a line and are connected.

Nomadic A way of life in which people travel from place to place.

North America One of the seven continents, located in the Northern Hemisphere.

Plain A wide expanse of mostly flat grassland with few trees.

Plateau A flat, raised area.

Rainforest A forest found in the tropical or temperate zones that is characterized by high humidity and high rainfall.

Replica A copy of an original.

Research station A place or building where scientific research is carried out.

Ruins The fallen or destroyed remains of a structure, such as a building or city.

Satellite A device sent into space that travels around Earth and collects information or helps with communication.

Savanna A type of grassland found in the tropical zone.

Settlement A community of people that live together.

Society A group of people who live and work together.

South America One of the seven continents, located primarily in the Southern Hemisphere.

Territory An area that belongs to another country.

Tourism Traveling for fun and adventure.

Tropical One of the world's climate zones, known for very hot and humid weather.

Tundra An area of land with no trees, not many plants, and a layer of permanently frozen soil—usually found in the Arctic regions or high on mountaintops.

Unpopulated Uninhabited, where no people live.

Volcanologist A scientist who studies and monitors volcanoes.

Index

Acknowledgments

The publisher would like to thank the following for
their kind permission to reproduce their photographs:

(Key: a-above; b-below/bottom; c-center; f-far; l-left; r-right; t-top)

123RF.com: Andreas Altenburger 27br, Olga Khoroshunova / goodolga 27tr, Margret Meyer 14-15bc; **Adobe Stock**: Donatas Dabravolskas 12b, Felix Mizioznikov 9tl; **Alamy Stock Photo**: Tatiana Aksenova 6bc, Anton Aleksenko 16-17c, AsiaDreamPhoto 26-27tc, Associated Press / Carlos Sanchez 10-11b, Associated Press / Mika Otsuki 13t, Aaron Asterley 28cra, Eyal Bartov 4bc, Andrey Gudkov / Biosphoto 15br, Raphael Sane / Biosphoto 31tr, Blue Jean Images 25tr, Joerg Boethling 29tr, Rosemary Calvert 5clb, Kike Calvo 13br, 42, Francis Cassidy 5cra, Cavan Images 6-7b, Design Pics Inc / David Kirkland / Axiom 29b, Werner Dieterich 18-19t, Colin Harris / era-images 32t, Galaxiid 29tl, 32b, Philip Game 28b, Brusini Auržlien / Hemis.fr 37br, Della Huff 15tr, Image Professionals GmbH / Hauke Dressler 28clb, imageBROKER.com GmbH & Co. KG / Fabian von Poser 24bc, imageBROKER.com GmbH & Co. KG / J & C Sohns 14clb, imageBROKER.com GmbH & Co. KG / Josef Beck 22-23tc, Iophius 36b, mauritius images GmbH / Hans Blossey 5tr, Galen Rowell / Mountain Light 33b, Christian Musat 30crb, Eric Nathan 13bl, Nature Picture Library / Nick Upton 37tl, NOAA 36cra, NPS Photo 9tr, 37tr, Anne Fritzenwanker / oneworld picture 9br, Operation 2022 8tr, Realimage 5tl, RGB Ventures / SuperStock / Brad Lewis 37bl, robertharding / Hans-Peter Merten 16cb, robertharding / Michael Nolan 6tr, ronnybas 5br, Grant Rooney 21br, Forray Didier / Sagaphoto.com 9bl, SOPA Images Limited 24cra, David South 33t, Tierfotoagentur / M. Zindl 23br, travellinglight 25tl, Wim Wiskerke 35bl, Zoonar / Pius Lee 16bl; **Depositphotos Inc**: storyteller2k20 17tr; **Dreamstime.com**: Alexlmx 34br, Wael Alreweie 35tl, Andrey Armyagov 34b, Ivan Bastien 18-19bc, Jaap Bleijenberg 12cra, Volodymyr Byrdyak 17br, Cmlndm 39br, Ryan Fletcher 35br, Peter Hermes Furian 8b, Paul Hampton 14-15tc, Vladislav Jirousek 22-23bc, Jmrocek 19tr, Tomas Marek 20bc, Mariusz Prusaczyk 4clb, 10-11tc, 16tc, Andrey Moisseyev 27cr, Luciano Mortula / Masterlu 6-7t, Nicolaforenza 21t, Ondrej Prosicky 18crb, Roberto Caucino / Rcaucino 11tr, Vladimir Seliverstov 31br, Sofiaworld 25b, Joa Souza 12clb, Staphy 30-31tc, 31bl, Ron Sumners / Sumnersgraphicsinc 26-27bc, Surasak Suwanmake 34cra, Víc V. 35tr, Xantana 21bl; **Getty Images**: Dhwee 19br, Stone / Peter Adams 43; **Getty Images / iStock**: alxpin 7br, Leonid Andronov 20b, benedek 20cra, Gregory_DUBUS 41br, JulieanneBirch 24b, nicolamargaret 10ca, sonatali 23tr, Rafael_Wiedenmeier 22clb, wsfurlan 10bc; **Shutterstock.com**: gpointstudio 17cr

Cover images: *Front*: **123RF.com**: Bogdan Serban br; **Dreamstime.com**: Roberto Caucino / Rcaucino bl; **Shutterstock.com**: Flash Vector t, Malchevska cr; *Back*: **Alamy Stock Photo**: Rosemary Calvert bl; **Dreamstime.com**: Andrey Moisseyev cl; **Getty Images**: Dhwee tl